The Great Narwhal Rescue

Saving the Arctic Ocean's Narwhals

Sandra Markle

Millbrook Press • Minneapolis

For Justin Hazard and all the students of Westwood Community School in Sloan, Iowa.

Acknowledgments: The author would like to thank the following people for sharing their enthusiasm and expertise: Dr. Susanna Blackwell, Greeneridge Sciences, Santa Barbara, California; Dr. Eva Garde, Greenland Institute of Natural Resources, University of Greenland, Nuuk, Greenland; Dr. Jens C. Koblitz, BioAcoustics Network, Neuss, Germany; Dr. Kristin Laidre, Polar Science Center, University of Washington, Seattle, Washington; Dr. Marianne Marcoux, Fisheries and Oceans Canada, Ottawa, Ontario, Canada; and Dr. Outi Tervo, Greenland Institute of Natural Resources, University of Greenland, Nuuk, Greenland.

A special thank-you to Skip Jeffery for his loving support during the creative process.

Text copyright © 2025 by Sandra Markle

All rights reserved. International copyright secured. No part of this book may be reproduced, stored in a retrieval system, or transmitted in any form or by any means—electronic, mechanical, photocopying, recording, or otherwise—without the prior written permission of Lerner Publishing Group, Inc., except for the inclusion of brief quotations in an acknowledged review.

Millbrook Press™
An imprint of Lerner Publishing Group, Inc.
241 First Avenue North
Minneapolis, MN 55401 USA

For reading levels and more information, look up this title at www.lernerbooks.com.

Maps on pages 19 and 22 by Laura K. Westlund.

Designed by Viet Chu.
Main body text set in Metro Office. Typeface provided by Linotype AG.

Library of Congress Cataloging-in-Publication Data

Names: Markle, Sandra, author.
Title: The great narwhal rescue : saving the Arctic ocean's narwhals / by Sandra Markle.
Description: Minneapolis : Millbrook Press, [2025] | Series: Sandra Markle's science discoveries | Includes bibliographical references and index. | Audience: Ages 9-12 | Audience: Grades 4-6 | Summary: "Narwhals have lived in the icy Arctic Ocean for centuries. But as temperatures rise, ice disappears, and humans venture into the Arctic, these animals are in danger. Discover how scientists are working to protect narwhals" —Provided by publisher.
Identifiers: LCCN 2024019398 (print) | LCCN 2024019399 (ebook) | ISBN 9798765610169 (library binding) | ISBN 9798765659311 (epub)
Subjects: LCSH: Narwhal—Arctic Ocean—Juvenile literature. | Narwhal—Conservation—Arctic Ocean—Juvenile literature.
Classification: LCC QL737.C433 M348 2025 (print) | LCC QL737.C433 (ebook) | DDC 599.5/43—dc23/eng/20240726

LC record available at https://lccn.loc.gov/2024019398
LC ebook record available at https://lccn.loc.gov/2024019399

Manufactured in the United States of America
1-1010934-51690-10/25/2024

TABLE OF CONTENTS

A Whale of a Beginning — 4
The Big Problem — 6
Time to Test — 14
Why All the Noise? — 18
New Risks in Once Safe Places — 21
A Race against Change — 27
Into a Hopeful Future — 34

A Note from Sandra Markle – 36

Did You Know? – 37

Glossary – 38

Source Notes – 39

Find Out More – 39

Index – 40

A WHALE OF A BEGINNING

Late one summer night, a narwhal pushed his head out of the water in East Greenland's Scoresby Sound near the North Pole. The young male didn't linger to take in the view. He was hungry and had only surfaced to breathe. He quickly dived back down, down, down into the inky depths. It was too dark underwater for his eyes to see, but that didn't stop him from swimming boldly forward. Even in the dark, he could sense what was around him and locate the fish he was hunting. Swimming fast despite his one damaged fin, he caught up to his dinner. The narwhal gulped down mouthful after mouthful of Arctic cod until his keen hearing picked up an unfamiliar sound. He stopped feeding and listened.

A narwhal is one of the deepest diving whales. An adult can hold its breath and stay underwater for about twenty-five minutes.

This sound was nothing like the swoosh of undersea currents, the rumble of an ice sheet breaking, or the distant thunder of an iceberg rolling and crashing into waves. He quickly returned to the surface where he could easily breathe while he swam away from whatever threat was making that noise. But once near the surface, the young male narwhal swam into a net. He flopped and struggled but couldn't break free. He was *trapped*!

Scientists conduct aerial surveys of the total narwhal population by using planes or drones to fly over groups and count individuals. Then they add the group totals together.

THE BIG PROBLEM

As of 2023, the scientists studying narwhals estimated the overall population to be about 173,000. Based on that total, the International Union for the Conservation of Nature (IUCN) listed the narwhals' status as Least Concern. That indicates the population is not considered at risk of becoming extinct, or no longer existing. But this classification isn't completely accurate.

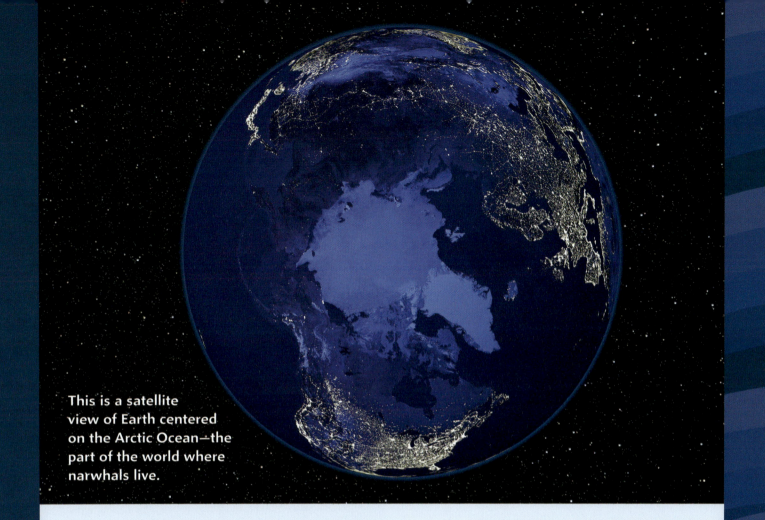

This is a satellite view of Earth centered on the Arctic Ocean—the part of the world where narwhals live.

Scientists believe some parts of the narwhal population are already endangered. That is because narwhals live in the Arctic Ocean. And narwhals live in groups, called pods, that migrate to spend their summers in one location and their winters in another. They also return to precisely the same locations by the same migration routes annually. Susanna Blackwell, an expert on marine mammals with Greeneridge Sciences in Santa Barbara, California, explained, "Even though, overall, the narwhal population is okay, the East Greenland population is in deep trouble. At this point, there are likely only about four hundred of that population remaining."

The East Greenland population is the narwhal pod that spends every summer in East Greenland's Scoresby Sound and migrates to overwinter in the Greenland Sea. But why is that population shrinking? And could whatever is wrong eventually cause the entire narwhal population to decrease? Maybe even become endangered? To find out, scientists needed to learn more about what was affecting the East Greenland narwhals.

MEET THE NARWHAL

A narwhal is a species, or kind, of whale. Like all whales, they live in ocean water but must surface to breathe air. The females give birth to babies that at first feed on their mother's milk. Whales are carnivores—animals that catch and eat other living things to survive. But how whales eat separates them into two groups: those with baleen (sievelike plates to filter food out of the water) and those with teeth. Narwhals are a species of toothed whales. Unlike other toothed whales, narwhals swallow their food whole. That's because they have only two teeth, and these can't be used to bite or chew. In most females, both teeth remain embedded in their gums. Most males have one tooth—rarely two—that emerges from the gum and grows through the upper lip to become a tusk.

FLUKES
These are two parts of the tail. They move up and down for swimming.

BODY
It is torpedo-shaped to slip easily through the water. Males are larger than females and may be up to 17 feet (5.2 m) long and weigh up to 2,000 pounds (907 kg).

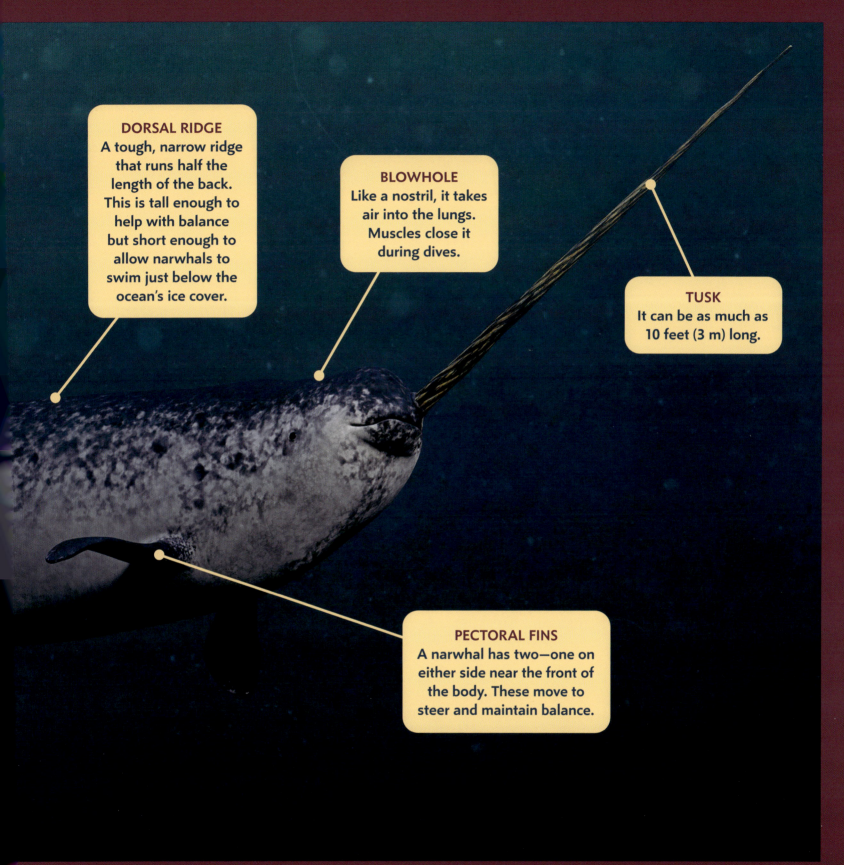

A combined group of scientists from the Greenland Institute of Natural Resources and the University of Copenhagen proposed a hypothesis as to why the East Greenland narwhal population was at risk. A hypothesis is a possible explanation that can be tested. And the scientists wanted to test the possibility that these narwhals were at risk because of human-made underwater noise pollution. They suspected that possibility because three sources of underwater noises were being introduced in the narwhals' environment: engine sounds from increased Arctic Ocean ship traffic, seismic sounding from searching for new oil and gas deposits, and underwater construction noises from building new oil well and wind turbine platforms. If human-made noise pollution was the problem, the scientists would need to figure out how to stop or reduce it to help narwhals.

These fishing trawlers near Greenland are just part of the increased ship traffic narwhals are encountering due to decreased Arctic Ocean ice.

HEARING IS ALSO SEEING

Although they have eyes and can see when there is enough light, narwhals can also sense whatever is around them when it is too dark to see. To do that, a narwhal inhales air through its blowhole while at the surface. Then, while underwater, the narwhal shifts the air from its lungs back and forth across special internal parts to produce clicks—as many as one thousand per second. It projects the clicks forward through a fatty part inside its forehead, called the melon. That amplifies and blasts out the clicks. Like an adjustable flashlight, narwhals dial down their blasts of clicks to a very narrow beam to sense something precisely. And they dial the blasts of clicks the other way to sense more broadly. Echoes bounce back from whatever the clicks strike. When these are picked up by fat pads on the narwhal's lower jaw, they are transmitted to its ears, which send signals to its brain. Once its brain interprets these signals, the narwhal senses whatever bounced back the echoes. Using sound this way to sense what is in the environment is called echolocation.

A narwhal calf sticks close to its mother as they travel together.

Keeping the local narwhal population healthy is important for all living things sharing their Arctic Ocean environment. Narwhals are a keystone species—their presence is essential to the health of the ecosystem. They hold that role because as top predators, they eat enough large and medium-sized Arctic fish and squid to keep those populations in check. And in turn that allows for an adequate plankton population. Plankton are the microscopic plants and animals, which form the foundational food source for all the food chains in the oceans.

The scientists chose Scoresby Sound on the eastern coast of Greenland as the site to test whether human-made noise pollution had any negative effect on narwhals. This area had few people living nearby and had, so far, remained largely free of ship traffic. That meant the narwhals that came annually to spend summers here had not been exposed to much human-made noise. But before they could do the testing, the scientists needed to establish a baseline of what were normal underwater noises in Scoresby Sound. They also needed to learn what was normal for a narwhal—both physically and behaviorally.

Each captured narwhal was quickly untangled from the net, and a strap around its tail anchored it in shallow water. Outi Tervo (Oh-TEE TER-voh) calms the narwhal while other members of the science team prepare to attach data-collecting instruments to its back.

To protect narwhals, only Indigenous people are legally permitted to hunt them for food and to continue cultural traditions. So, the scientists had to contract with local hunters to catch the narwhals that would be their test subjects. Next, they needed to attach instruments to record information about each narwhal's reactions during the tests. Because the instruments were numbered, they could have used those for identification. Instead, they chose to name each narwhal. Outi Tervo from the Greenland Institute of Natural Resources said, "It's easier to keep track of individuals if they have a proper name." And the scientists frequently chose names from Norse mythology, such as Aegir and Helge.

All the test instruments were attached to a narwhal's back by suction cups. To create the baseline for their study, the scientists attached an Acousonde. This sound recording device recorded any noises the narwhal made as well as any noises around it in Scoresby Sound. Other instruments monitored the narwhal's heart rate and breathing rate. A satellite transmitter monitored its location. The scientists also anchored hydrophones (microphones that pick up sound waves underwater) on the seafloor and on drifting floats. For seven summers (2010 through 2016), they monitored six narwhals (a mix of males and females depending on what were caught each year) for up to seven days. Once they compiled all the data, they had established what were normal underwater noises in Scoresby Sound. And they understood what was normal for a narwhal—both physically and behaviorally. It was time to add some underwater noise pollution and see how narwhals responded.

Susanna Blackwell holds an Acousonde like the one used in the study. This, like all the instruments in the study, was attached to each test narwhal's back by suction cups. After a week or two, the ocean's salt water gradually dissolved magnesium connectors, which released the suction cups so the instruments slid off. Once the instruments floated up, they emitted signals that let the scientists find them and study the recorded data.

The research vessel *Paamiut* in Scoresby Sound

TIME TO TEST

In the summer of 2017, the scientists started testing how narwhals reacted when exposed to human-made noises in their home environment. To do that, they had the assistance of the Danish Greenland Institute of Natural Resources vessel *Paamiut* (paw-MUTE). So, once the monitoring instruments were attached to that year's six test narwhals (all males), the ship sailed around and around in Scoresby Sound. In addition to its engine noises, the ship used a seismic air gun to blast bursts of pressurized air into the water, which created more sounds for the narwhals to experience.

After the data-collecting instruments detached, floated up, and were recovered, the scientists analyzed the results. The satellite transmitter let them know where each narwhal was when it experienced the seismic air gun pulses and pair that with its physical responses. The data revealed that each of the narwhals reacted to the noise pollution with changed heart rates and breathing rates. The narwhals also responded by swimming away from the noise and heading toward shallower water—a typical narwhal escape response to danger. That is a good response if the threat is a killer whale because those narwhal predators are bigger and require deeper water for swimming than narwhals. But the narwhals could not escape from noise pollution.

The next stage of testing was to find out how narwhals reacted to stronger noises closer to the level human activities were creating. So, during the summer of 2018, the scientists returned to Scoresby Sound to conduct more tests. One by one, the five test narwhals caught by Indigenous hunters were outfitted with the testing instruments. This time, these included an Acousonde, a dive depth recorder, and monitors for heart rate, breathing rate, and fluke stroking rate (speed of up and down tail movement). They also attached two satellite transmitters to each narwhal to closely track movements and record locations during each testing period.

While the scientists were attaching instruments to one male narwhal for that summer's test, they realized they had monitored it before. The scar pattern on its back and especially its one damaged pectoral fin let them know this was a narwhal they had named Nemo during the 2014 baseline studies. Since they had recorded how Nemo reacted to the normal noises in Scoresby Sound, they were especially interested to learn how he responded to the noise pollution.

The loop around its tail anchors the narwhal. The scientists keep it afloat so it can breathe while they work quickly to attach the data-recording instruments.

Some of the scientists who attached the data-collecting instruments returned to their laboratories to await test results. Others joined the scientists already on board the HDMS *Lauge Koch* (LAOW-guh coke), which was participating in this year's study. Then, for seven days—August 25 through September 1, 2018—the scientists used the test narwhals' locations relayed by their satellite transmitters to make sure they were within listening range. And during testing, the ship fired a seismic air gun every eighty seconds at a depth of about 19 feet (6 m) for a maximum of five hours. In between tests, the ship refrained from firing and shut down its engines, so the narwhals were only exposed to Scoresby Sound's typical noises.

After the weeklong test, the instruments released from each of the study's narwhals. After the scientists retrieved those, they examined that summer's data. Tervo reported, "The narwhals' heart rates went both up and down. That was very surprising because it showed they were reacting very, very strongly and were very sensitive to the noise—even quite far away." What concerned the scientists wasn't whether the narwhals' heart rate increased or slowed.

This is the Royal Danish Navy vessel P-572 HDMS *Lauge Koch* photographed near Nuuk, Greenland. This ship created noise pollution in Scoresby Sound during the 2018 tests.

The science team attached instruments to each test narwhal. Nemo's Acousonde was attached on August 24 and stayed on for six days. After scientists retrieved it, Blackwell discovered it contained recordings of more than 110 hours.

It was that this reaction showed how very sensitive they were to the noise pollution. Even without the seismic air gun pulses, from as much as 25 miles (40 km) away, the narwhals showed a response to just the engine and propeller noises when the ship was moving.

After studying the results from each of the test narwhals, Blackwell expressed surprise at Nemo's reactions. She said, "He was just hyper whale!" The data collected from Nemo's instruments showed he was physically stressed both while near the ship and whenever the seismic gun pulsed. On August 26, the second day of testing, as soon as the seismic air gun pulsed, Nemo raced toward shallower water—that typical narwhal escape response. But Nemo's actions didn't help him escape. He swam right into a local hunter's net. Fortunately the hunter spotted the instruments on Nemo's back and immediately released him to rejoin the test group.

WHY ALL THE NOISE?

The noise problem in the Arctic region is happening because it's warming up. For millions of years, that northernmost part of the world was covered by ice much of the year. That blocked human activity. But warmer temperatures have been melting ice in the region. The National Snow and Ice Data Center reported that from the late 1970s to 2003, the Arctic area permanently covered by ice shrank by about 40 percent. In September 2023, following the summer months of melting, the ice-covered area of the Arctic Ocean was estimated to be no bigger than twice the size of Texas. That change has provided humans with never-before-possible access to areas the narwhals call home and opportunities for noisy activities.

It's no wonder that in just six years—from 2015 to 2021—scientists studying underwater human-made noise pollution in the Arctic Ocean reported it doubled. Tervo said, "For narwhals, the whole Arctic Ocean used to be as quiet as a faraway meadow where there was only an occasional passing car. Now, it's as noisy as someplace with nonstop rush hour traffic."

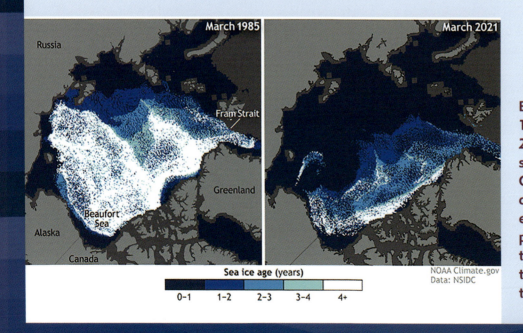

Between March 1985 and March 2021, the amount of sea ice in the Arctic Ocean decreased dramatically. And each year, less ice persists through the year, leading to thinner ice covering the water.

Increased human access to the Arctic region is not just intruding on narwhals where they spend their summers. Eva Garde with the Greenland Institute of Natural Resources said, "GPS tracking of narwhals has revealed they not only spend every summer of their lives in the same area. They also migrate to the same area every winter." Migrating narwhals so faithfully follow the same routes between their summer and winterover locations that Indigenous people report seeing narwhals pass their villages at the same time every year. And such exact annual travels means narwhals are at risk of experiencing human-made noise pollution in different areas.

Decisions about human access to the Arctic Circle are made by these countries. They claim political control over the region.

LIVING THE TRAVELING LIFE

By tracking the yearly travels of narwhals, scientists discovered they are creatures of habit. They are forever faithful to summering in the shallow bay, sound, or fjord where they were born. They also follow specific routes at the same times each year to travel between their summer home and where they spend the winter. Wherever they live or travel, narwhals are always part of a pod.

Tervo said, "Very little is known about the social structure of narwhals [in pods]. But they do form big aggregations [clusters] and within these we see pods of males plus separate pods of young males and pods of females with young." In late September to early November, many narwhals merge into super pods made up of as many as a thousand individuals. That is when mating occurs. But for much of the year, narwhals remain in smaller pods, which may be as few as two to ten individuals.

Males and females mate from late September to early November. At that time each year lots of narwhals gather together.

NEW RISKS IN ONCE SAFE PLACES

The narwhals from Canada and West Greenland spend April to September or November in northern, ice-free coastal areas, such as Scoresby Sound. In late September to mid-November, they migrate south to winter in the Greenland Sea or in the Baffin Bay–Davis Strait area between Canada and western Greenland. Scientists mapped the precise seasonal locations and annual travels of these narwhals and other regional groups. From that, they determined where and how increased human access to the Arctic Ocean was most impacting the narwhal population.

From the air, older ice looks white and thinner, still-forming winter ice looks pale grayish blue. Don't miss the narwhal that has surfaced to breathe.

Because they are so perfectly suited to living with ice, narwhals are suffering where the Arctic Ocean has already lost its ice cover. Even where the surface remains covered, the ice is often thinner than in the past, allowing increased human access and causing problems for narwhals.

The photo at right shows the US Coast Guard ship *Healy* in 2012 helping the Russian tanker *Renda* cross the Arctic Ocean by breaking ice around it. The strong double hull construction and ability to power through ice makes icebreakers suited to clearing a path for other ships. At first, such Arctic crossings, even with icebreaker assistance, were only possible during summers. But cargo ships increasingly took this shortcut between Europe and Asia, called the Northwest Passage (*shown below*). It let ships make the trip as much as fifteen days faster than the previous route, which required going through the Suez Canal in Egypt.

Shipping Routes between Western Europe and Eastern Asia

- - - - Northwest Passage
——— Suez Route

By 2014 both the amount of sea ice and its thickness were greatly reduced. Ships needed only reinforced hulls (bands of metal wrapped around the outside and metal sheeting added to the bow and stern) to make the Arctic Ocean crossing year-round. So, a steadily increasing number of cargo ships and tankers used the Northwest Passage.

Greatly reduced year-round ice cover also let killer whales—narwhal predators—access Admiralty Inlet near Baffin Island during the summer months when many female narwhals were there with calves. Previously, because killer whales, like narwhals, need to surface to breathe, their tall dorsal fins prevented them from having easy access to openings in the ice cover, so they stayed away.

These killer whales swim in open water next to a sheet of sea ice.

To fully evaluate how the Northwest Passage being open was impacting sea traffic, the Arctic Council's Protection of the Arctic Marine Environment group counted the number of ships using this route between 2013 and 2019. The results showed a 44 percent increase during just those six years. The scientists knew those chugging cargo ships put narwhals in danger of being struck and suffering cuts, broken bones, or fatal wounds. They also knew the ship traffic greatly increased underwater noise pollution.

Reduced ice coverage year-round in the Arctic Ocean has also allowed increased commercial fishing. These fishing vessels are in the northern Barents Sea area of the Arctic Ocean. They are mainly catching Arctic cod—one of the narwhal's main food sources. This is not yet causing food shortages for narwhals, but it could.

In addition to using the Northwest Passage for shipping, countries with land claims within the Arctic Circle were eager to harvest oil and natural gas deposits. The US Geological Survey estimated that as much as 22 percent of the world's remaining untapped oil and gas deposits were in that region. Those natural resources formed over millions of years as lots of living things died and settled to the bottom of the ocean. There, the remains decayed and were buried under sediment that piled up and packed together. Shifting sediment layers created great pressure and heat, transforming the decayed remains into oil or gas. Now, with the diminished ice cover, companies were eager to start testing using seismic air guns to locate these petroleum resources and then construct drilling platforms.

On August 2, 2007, this miniature submarine was lowered from a Russian ship into the Arctic Ocean at Earth's North Pole. Once it reached the seafloor, a mechanical arm dropped a rustproof titanium version of the Russian flag, claiming the area and any resources existing there for Russia. But, as of 2023, the other Arctic region countries assert this region is largely in international waters and cannot belong to any one country.

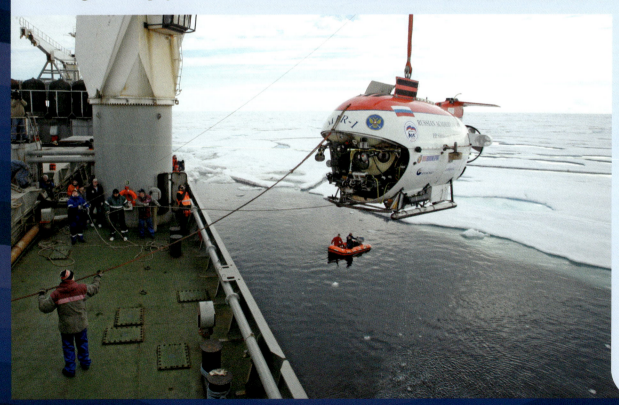

This is the 2020 test model of a floating wind turbine manufactured by Aerodyn Engineering.

Decreased ice cover opened the Arctic Ocean for yet another noisy human activity—building wind turbines to produce electricity. Scientists developed a way for wind turbines to float on platforms anchored by chains instead of sitting atop tall towers built up from the seafloor. That made it possible to build wind turbines in deep ocean water to take advantage of strong, persistent winds across such areas. In 2022, Norway, for example, launched seven floating wind turbines and added four more in 2023. But such deepwater locations are also where narwhals hunt for fish along the seafloor.

The study of the already shrinking population in Scoresby Sound proved that even a ship's engine noise was enough to stress out some hypersensitive whales, such as Nemo. So, although increasing human access was likely to mean even more noise pollution, something had to be done to make the Arctic Ocean quieter again. But what?

A RACE AGAINST CHANGE

The Arctic Circle countries have officially agreed that some part of the Arctic Ocean and its coastal areas should be reserved as safe places for narwhals and other Arctic wildlife. But as of 2020, less than 5 percent of the Arctic Ocean had any form of protected-area status.

Meanwhile, Canada is attempting to make the Baffin Bay–Davis Strait area a quiet zone for the part of the narwhal population that winters there. As of 2023, most noisy human activities were restricted in that area. But for narwhals to continue to thrive in the Arctic Ocean, just trying to block out human activity in some areas won't be enough. With steadily decreasing ice cover, steadily increasing human use of the Arctic is inevitable. The answer must be to find ways to make those activities quieter.

Look closely and you'll see each surfacing narwhal's blowhole. A narwhal needs only enough open water space to get its blowhole above water to breathe. It exhales stale air from its lungs, blasting water out of the way. Then it takes a big, deep breath to fill its lungs before it dives again.

As early as 2008, the National Oceanic and Atmospheric Administration (NOAA) urged ships to reduce their speed in certain parts of the Arctic Ocean at certain times of the year for migrating narwhals and other marine life. Slower ships produce less disturbing engine and propeller noises. And conservation groups are urging NOAA to limit the use of the Northwest Passage to only those ships powered by electric engines, which are much quieter than fossil fuel engines or steam engines. But that has not happened. Nor have ships regularly slowed down while navigating the Northwest Passage. Going slower makes trips take longer, and that makes shipping costs more expensive.

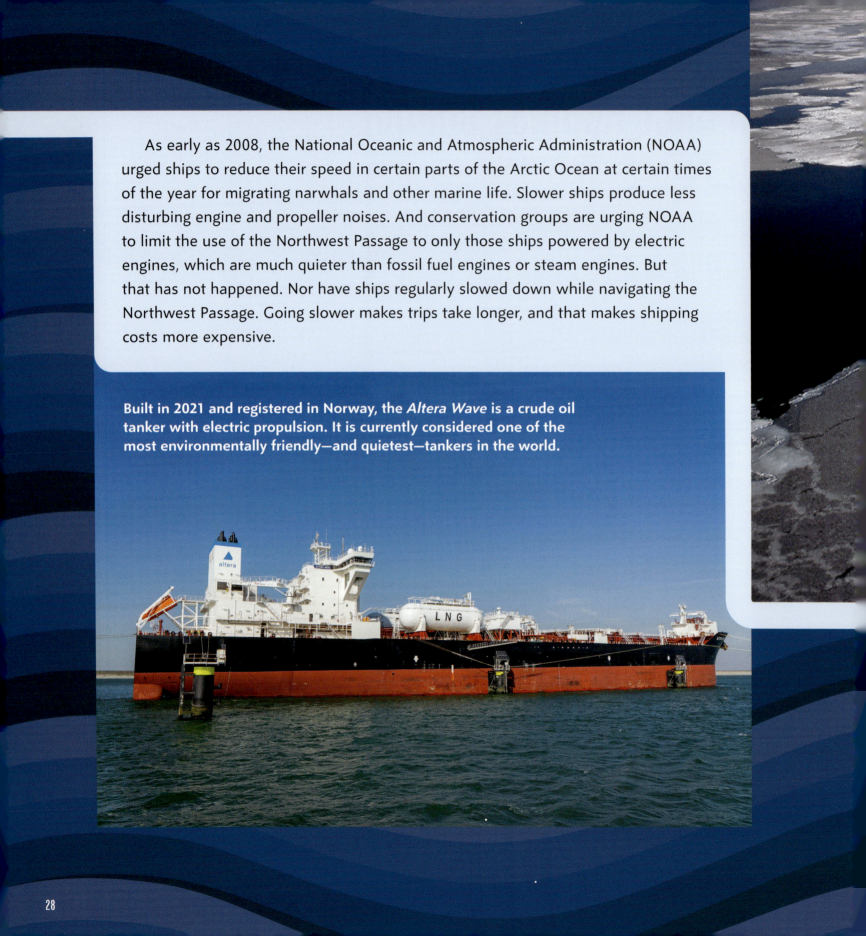

Built in 2021 and registered in Norway, the *Altera Wave* is a crude oil tanker with electric propulsion. It is currently considered one of the most environmentally friendly—and quietest—tankers in the world.

This ship in the Arctic Ocean is conducting noisy seismic testing for oil and gas deposits.

Seismic air gun pulses used during oil and gas exploration may travel a very long distance from the source. Ocean platform construction and operation also generate underwater noise pollution that extends as far as 10 miles (16 km) from the site. Luckily, there is a solution to both of these sources of noise pollution—bubbles. A bubble barrier can contain any noise inside a very small area. This works for the same reason that you can barely hear someone above water yelling while you are underwater. Sound waves lose a lot of energy when they travel between air and water.

The method for producing an underwater bubble barrier, or wall of bubbles, was originally developed in the 1940s by Dutch engineers. It was designed to block salty ocean water from entering freshwater canals used to irrigate growing crops. The German company Hydrotechnik Lübeck (WHO-droh-tek-nik LOO-bek) worked with this idea to develop the modern version they named the Big Bubble Barrier. A flexible, perforated (full of holes) hose or multiple hoses are anchored to the seafloor encircling a construction site. Each hose is connected to pumps on a ship or platform at the surface. The bubbles are created when air is pumped through the hose. The wall of bubbles rises all the way to the surface. That creates a barrier that blocks any sound waves generated inside the wall. Hydrotechnik Lübeck's tests indicated that as much as 95 percent of any noises produced inside the Big Bubble Barrier stay inside.

The flexible hose or hoses surrounding a drilling platform or wind turbine platform form an effective noise barrier during construction and operation. That's because there are many holes, letting compressed air pumped through the hose escape, rise, and form a wall of bubbles.

The *Blue Aries* is the ship outside the double Big Bubble Barrier. It supplies the compressed air used to create the underwater walls of bubbles. Multiple walls create an even better sound barrier.

These narwhals are sharing an ice break to breathe. But when climate changes cause sections of the Arctic Ocean's ice cover to shift unexpectantly, narwhals can become trapped.

These noise control efforts help improve underwater conditions in the Arctic Ocean. But global climate change is causing continued melting in the Arctic Ocean, opening it to even more human access and activities. And that is bad news for narwhals.

Narwhals are so uniquely, perfectly adapted to be at home in the cold, partly ice-covered ocean that they can't move to a new home elsewhere in the ocean. They have a thick layer of blubber (a special kind of fat) under their skin that is perfect for shielding them from the icy cold water but won't let them live in warm water. Narwhals also have diets limited to eating a limited variety of Arctic Ocean prey in specific areas at different times of the year. And they live long lives. Tervo said, "Narwhals live for maybe one hundred years or even more. So, it is likely [with continued climate change] they will experience big changes in their lifetime."

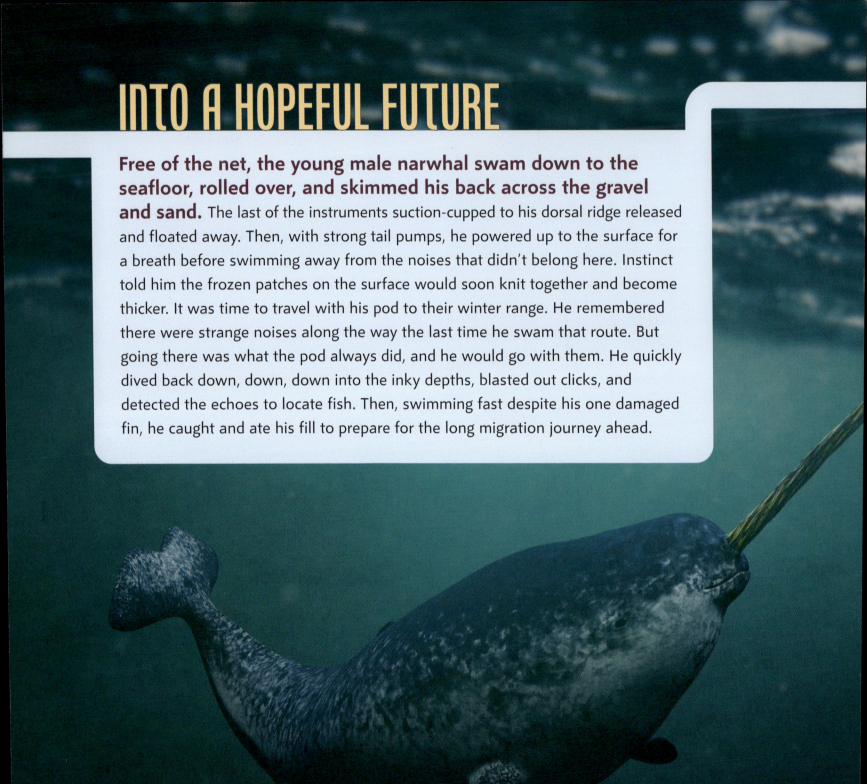

INTO A HOPEFUL FUTURE

Free of the net, the young male narwhal swam down to the seafloor, rolled over, and skimmed his back across the gravel and sand. The last of the instruments suction-cupped to his dorsal ridge released and floated away. Then, with strong tail pumps, he powered up to the surface for a breath before swimming away from the noises that didn't belong here. Instinct told him the frozen patches on the surface would soon knit together and become thicker. It was time to travel with his pod to their winter range. He remembered there were strange noises along the way the last time he swam that route. But going there was what the pod always did, and he would go with them. He quickly dived back down, down, down into the inky depths, blasted out clicks, and detected the echoes to locate fish. Then, swimming fast despite his one damaged fin, he caught and ate his fill to prepare for the long migration journey ahead.

Conservationists are striving hard to help narwhals' Arctic Ocean home remain the ecosystem they know and need. Tervo said, "It's important to manage the Arctic properly so the noise pollution and the human expansion [to use the Arctic's resources] will not be too costly for nature."

Wherever you live, even if it's far from the Arctic Ocean, you can join the conservation effort to help narwhals. It is as simple as using less electricity, traveling less in gasoline-powered vehicles, and consuming fewer products shipped in from faraway places. It may seem impossible that one person can help. But each one joining in this effort will gradually lead to many participating. And one day in the future, who knows what conservation effort you might work with to make a difference. What new invention you might create to help make human activities in the Arctic Ocean quieter. Or what new knowledge your research might discover to help ensure the Arctic Ocean remains where narwhals can live in peace—*and quiet*— as a healthy keystone species for that unique environment.

A Note from Sandra Markle

I *love* research! Digging up information is my kind of treasure hunt. Even better is tracking down experts around the world and talking with them about their research. Best is when they share a discovery that has only recently been made. Lights flash, bells ring—well, in my imagination. I whip out my trusty laptop, settle on the sofa wearing my favorite slippers, and charge into more research.

That is exactly what happened when I interviewed narwhal expert Kristin Laidre about the narwhal's tusk for a different book. She shared news that a science team in Greenland's Scoresby Sound had recently done tests on narwhals by catching some, attaching data-collecting instruments, and then firing off seismic air guns underwater from a nearby ship. She said that learning about the effect of noise pollution on narwhals was a breakthrough for helping the whole population, though narwhals in some areas were already in deep trouble. That was the beginning of my research adventure tracking down experts to learn exactly how the Scoresby Sound noise pollution tests were done, what they revealed, and how those discoveries are powering up efforts to help narwhals there and throughout the Arctic Ocean. I will definitely be continuing to follow and support efforts to help narwhals. And I will always be hopeful for their future!

Did You Know?

A narwhal is the only tusked animal whose tusk is straight rather than curved. It is also spiraled. Scientists believe males use their tusks to compete for mates. But males have only been observed dueling with gentle tusk rubs.

Females usually give birth to a single calf—very rarely twins—every three years. The calf develops inside its mother's body for about fourteen months, and most are born in the Arctic spring (April through May). The calf nurses and stays close to its mother for at least a year.

Narwhals change color as they age. Calves are mainly gray, juveniles are bluish black, mature adults are spotty gray, and older narwhals are almost completely white.

Narwhals are among the deepest diving whales and dive to the ocean floor primarily to hunt for fish, such as halibut. The deepest recorded narwhal dive was 5,827 feet (1,776 m).

A narwhal sleeps often but only for ten to thirty minutes at a time, which lets it keep surfacing to breathe. And a narwhal only rests half its brain at a time, so it keeps swimming and stays alert to possible danger while sleeping.

Glossary

adult: a narwhal once it is able to reproduce. A female usually becomes an adult once she is five to eight years old; a male usually becomes an adult when he is eleven to thirteen years old. An adult narwhal may live to be one hundred years old—or even older.

aerial survey: a method of collecting information about something on Earth's surface using drones or airplanes

blowhole: the opening that is the nostril for breathing on the top of a narwhal's head

blubber: a thick layer of fat directly under the narwhal's skin

calf: a narwhal from birth until it is about twenty months old

echolocation: the ability to project sounds and evaluate the returning echoes to sense an environment

ecosystem: plants and animals that share a specific environment and interact with one another and all the nonliving things in that environment, including water, dirt, rocks, and sun

fluke: each of the two sections of a narwhal's tail

juvenile: a narwhal from about twenty months old until it's old enough to reproduce

keystone species: a living thing—usually an animal—on which other living things in that ecosystem depend and without it the ecosystem would be very different

melon: the fatty structure inside the narwhal's forehead that projects the sounds it produces forward

migration: seasonal movement from one region to another

pod: a social group of narwhals

predator: an animal that catches and eats other animals

prey: an animal caught as food by another animal

sea ice: frozen seawater that floats on the surface of the ocean

seismic air gun: a device that produces pressurized blasts of air and is often used in the ocean to penetrate the seafloor when exploring for oil and gas deposits

super pod: a very large pod of narwhals formed by smaller pods merging. This regularly happens for seasonal migrations.

tusk: an enlarged narwhal tooth most commonly found in males

Source Notes

7   Susanna Blackwell, interview with the author, August 26, 2022.

13 Outi Tervo, interview with the author, August 9, 2022.

16 Tervo.

17 Blackwell, interview.

18 Tervo, interview.

19 Eva Garde, interview with the author, August 12, 2022.

20 Tervo, interview.

21 Garde, interview.

33 Tervo, interview.

35 Tervo.

Find Out More

Check out these books and websites to discover even more:

CBC Kids News: What Do Narwhals Sound Like?
https://www.youtube.com/watch?v=i71d8qU8V1g
Listen to recordings of narwhals making sounds. And find out why they make these different sounds.

Discover Wildlife: Narwhal Guide
https://www.discoverwildlife.com/animal-facts/mammals/narwhal-guide/
Discover lots of fun facts and great videos of narwhals in action.

Fleming, Candace. *Narwhal: Unicorn of the Arctic.* New York: Anne Schwartz Books, 2024. This beautifully illustrated text lets you experience a year in the life of a male narwhal from its point of view.

NASA: Global Climate Change Vital Sign of the Planet
https://climate.nasa.gov/explore/interactives/
This site is packed with fascinating, interactive ways to view how global climate change is affecting Earth's habitats. Don't miss the *Climate Time Machine* section.

Index

Acousonde, 13, 15
aerial survey, 6
Arctic Ocean traffic, 10, 12, 24

Baffin Bay–Davis Strait, 21, 27
Blackwell, Susanna, 7, 13, 17
bubble barrier, 29–31

Canada, 21, 27
climate change, 32–33

East Greenland narwhal population, 7, 10
echolocation, 11, 34

Garde, Eva, 19

Indigenous peoples, 13, 15, 19
International Union for the Conservation of Nature (ICUN), 6

maps, 18–19, 22
narwhal
 calves, 23
 diet, 4, 12, 24, 26, 33, 34
 habitat, 7, 8, 33
 migration, 7, 19, 21, 34
 threats, 5, 14, 23, 24
 tusk, 8–9
National Oceanic and Atmospheric Administration (NOAA), 28
Nemo, 15, 17, 26
noise pollution, 10, 12–19, 24, 26, 29, 35
Northwest Passage, 22–25, 28
Norway, 26, 28

oil drilling, 10, 25

Paamiut, 14
P-572 HDMS *Lauge Koch*, 16
Protection of the Arctic Marine Environment, 24

Scoresby Sound, 14–16, 21, 26
sea ice, 5, 10, 21–27, 32–33
seismic air gun, 14, 16–17, 25, 29
shipping routes, 22–24

Tervo, Outi, 12, 13, 16, 18, 20, 33, 35

wind turbine, 10, 26

Photo Acknowledgments

Image credits: A & J Visage/Alamy, pp. 1, 20, 27; dotted zebra/Alamy, pp. 4–5, 8–9; 34–35; Photo: Carsten Egevang, pp. 6, 12, 14, 15, 17; Science Photo Library/Alamy, p. 7; Justin Lewis/Getty Images, p. 10; Nature Picture Library/Alamy, p. 11; Marguerite Holloway, p. 13; Photo by Timothy Choi, p. 16; NOAA, p. 18; Kristin Laidre, p. 21; Stocktrek Images/Getty Images, p. 22; Design Pics Inc/Alamy, p. 23; piola666/Getty Images, p. 24; AP Photo/Vladimir Chistyakov, p. 25; Jens Büttner/picture alliance/Getty Images, p. 26; Jochen Tack /Alamy, p. 28; westphalia/Getty Images, p. 29; Hydrotechnik Lübeck GmbH, Germany, pp. 30, 31; © Flip Nicklin/Minden Pictures, pp. 32–33; Skip Jeffery Photography, p. 36; Todd Mintz Photography/Alamy, p. 37. Design elements: artvea/Getty Images.

Cover: dotted zebra/Alamy; Kristin Laidre.